Henry Edward Manning

The Daemon of Socrates

A Paper Read before the Royal Institution, Jan. 26, 1872

Henry Edward Manning

The Daemon of Socrates
A Paper Read before the Royal Institution, Jan. 26, 1872

ISBN/EAN: 9783337038816

Printed in Europe, USA, Canada, Australia, Japan

Cover: Foto ©Thomas Meinert / pixelio.de

More available books at **www.hansebooks.com**

THE

DÆMON OF SOCRATES.

LONDON : PRINTED BY
SPOTTISWOODE AND CO., NEW-STREET SQUARE
AND PARLIAMENT STREET

THE

DÆMON OF SOCRATES.

A PAPER

READ BEFORE

THE ROYAL INSTITUTION,

Jan. 26, 1872,

BY

HENRY EDWARD

ARCHBISHOP OF WESTMINSTER.

LONDON:

LONGMANS, GREEN, AND CO.

1872.

DÆMON OF SOCRATES.

AT THE OUTSET I must plead guilty to a misnomer,
for which, however, I am not responsible. It has
become a tradition to speak of the Dæmon of
Socrates; but I hope to show that the term is
without warrant and incorrect.

The Dæmon of Socrates has been treated so often,
and by so many authors, historians, philosophers, and
critics, both in classical and Christian times, that I,
at least, cannot hope to say anything new upon it.
I may, however, review the judgments of others, and
then offer what seems to me to be the true inter-
pretation of this singular fact in the history of
philosophy.

It will, I think, be found to be no mere intellectual eccentricity, no mere superstition, still less an
unmeaning record of Greek history, but a fact in
the psychology of the greatest philosophical mind

of the ancient world, full of significance for us, and
throwing much light upon the analysis of our moral
nature.

The life of Socrates extended over a tract of
seventy years, that is from 469 to 400 B.C., and
embraced the most critical and splendid period of
Athenian history.   During his lifetime, Athens rose
to the height of its imperial hegemony over the
states, and islands, and colonies of Greece; at the
time of his death its decline was already far ad-
vanced.   It was the period of the final victories over
the Persians, and also of the Peloponnesian contests.
In his day the Constitution of Athens passed from
its aristocratic period to the conflicts of democracy
and oligarchy, which completed its fall.   In Politics,
it was the time of Pericles, and of the statesmen
formed by him : in Philosophy, of the Hylozoists,
the Atomists, and the Metaphysical or Theological
Philosophers so ably described here last year by
Professor Blackie; and also of the Sophists : in
Poetry, of Sophocles and Aristophanes ; and in Arts,
of Phidias.

In the midst of all these splendours of imperial
greatness, intellectual culture, excessive refinement,
luxurious self-indulgence, public and private immo-
rality, Socrates arose as a cross-questioner of men,

a seeker after moral truth, an example and a teacher of temperance and justice. There is something majestic and melancholy in his account of himself, and of his mission, as he declared it in his Apology before his judges.

He was accused by Meletus and Anytus of corrupting the youth of Athens by philosophical paradoxes, and of introducing new gods, or of denying all gods. In answer he spoke as follows :

'If you should say to me, "O Socrates, we will not believe Anytus. We will let you off; but on this condition, that you no longer go on with this questioning and philosophising ; and if you should be caught again doing this, you shall die."

'If, as I said, you should acquit me on these conditions, I should say to you, O men of Athens, I reverence you and I love you, but I shall obey God rather than you. As long as I breathe, and am able, I shall not cease to philosophise, and to exhort you, and to demonstrate (the truth) to whomsoever among you I may light upon, saying, in my accustomed words, " How is it, O best of men, that you, being an Athenian, and of a city the greatest and noblest for wisdom and power, are not ashamed to be careful of money, studying how you can make the most of it; and of glory also and of honour: but of prudence, and truth, and of the soul, how you may make the best of that, have neither care nor thought?" 'And this I will do, to young and old, whomsoever I may meet; both to alien and citizen, and, above all, to the men of this city, inasmuch as you are nearer to me in kindred. For this is the command of God, as you well know: and I think that no greater good ever yet came to the State, than this service which I render to God. For I go about doing nothing else than to persuade you, both young and old, to be careful in the first place neither of the body, nor of money, nor of anything so earnestly as of the soul, how you may make it as perfect as possible. I tell you that virtue does not spring from money, but that from virtue money springs, and all other goods of man, both to the individual and to the common-wealth. If, then, to teach these things be to destroy our young men, that would be mischievous in me indeed. But if anyone should say I teach anything other than these truths, he speaks falsely. Moreover, I say, O Athenians, whether you believe Anytus or not, and whether you let me go or not, I shall never do anything else, even though I were to die many times.*

* Apologia Socratis, s. 17. Platonis Opp., vol. i. 114. Ed. Stallbaum, Gothæ, 1858.

'Do not clamour, O Athenians, but abide by the request I made to you, that is, not to clamour at what I am saying, but to hear me. For you will be benefited, I believe, by hearing me. I am about to say to you some things, at which, perhaps, you will cry out; but I pray you not to do so. For you know well, if you should kill me, being such a one as I say I am, you will not hurt me so much as you will hurt yourselves. Neither Meletus nor Anytus can any way hurt me. This cannot be. For I do not think that it is ever permitted that a better man should be hurt by a worse. Perhaps, indeed, he may kill him or drive him into exile, or disfranchise him; and these things perhaps he and others may think to be great evils. But I do not think so: much rather the doing that which he (Meletus) is now about—the laying hands on a man to kill him unjustly, is a great evil. But, O Athenians, I am far from making now a defence for myself, as some may think; [I am making it] in your behalf; lest by condemning me you should in anything offend in the matter of this gift which God has given you. For if you should kill me, you will not easily find another man like me, who, to speak in a comic way, is so precisely adapted by God to the State; which is like a horse, large and well-bred, but from its very size sluggish, and needing to be roused by some gad-fly. For so it seems to me, that the God has applied me, such as I am, to the State, that I may never cease to rouse you, and persuade and shame everyone, fastening upon you everywhere all day long. Such another will not easily come to you, O men of Athens; and if you will listen to me, you will spare me. But perhaps, as those who awake in anger when they are stung, you will, at the instigation of Anytus, kill me at once with a slap; then you will end the rest of your life in sleep, unless God shall send some other gad-fly to be mindful of you. But that I am such a one, given by God to the State, you may know from this fact. It is not like the way of men that I, now for so many years, should have disregarded all my own concerns, and should have endured the neglect of my own domestic affairs, and should have been ever busied about your interests; going about to each of you privately, as a father or an elder brother, persuading you to be careful of virtue. If indeed I had derived any enjoyment from these things, and for these exhortations had received any reward, there would have been some reason in it. But now you yourselves see that the accusers, charging me as they do, without shame, of other things, of this at least have not been able to bring a witness against me; as if I had ever either exacted or asked any reward. I think, moreover, that I adduce a sufficient witness that I speak the truth—I mean my poverty.' *

'It may perhaps appear strange that I should go to and fro, giving advice, and busying myself about these things in private, but that in public I should not venture to go up (i.e. to the Pnyx) to give counsel to the State before your assembly. But the cause of this is what you have heard me say often and in many places; that a voice is present with me —a certain agency of God, somewhat divine (δαιμό-νιον)—which indeed Meletus has caricatured and put into the indictment. Now this began with me from my childhood; a certain voice, which always, when it comes, turns me aside from that which I am about to do, but never impels me to do anything. It is this which opposed my mixing in politics, and I think very wisely. For you well know, O Athenians, that if I had been hitherto mixed in political matters, I should have perished long ago; and should have done no good, either to you or to myself. Do not be angry with me for speaking the truth; for there is no man who will save his life if he shall courageously oppose either you or any other popu-

* Ibid. s. 18, p. 118.

lace, by striving to hinder the multitude of unjust and lawless things which are done in the State. It is necessary, therefore, that anyone who really combats for the sake of justice, if he would survive even for a little while, should live a private and not a public life.' *

When Socrates had ended his defence, the votes were taken: first, he was condemned as guilty of the charges laid against him; and, secondly, he was sentenced to die. He then once more addressed the court.

'I would wish to speak kindly with those who have voted for me, in respect to what has now happened; while the archons are occupied, and before I go to the place where I must die. Bear with me, therefore, O Athenians, for such time as we have. While it is so permitted, nothing forbids our conversing together. I wish to show to you, as my friends, what is the meaning of that which has now befallen me. O my judges—for in calling you judges I should call you rightly—something marvellous has happened to me. Hitherto, the Oracle of the δαιμόνιον, which is familiarly about me, with great frequency has opposed itself, even in very little things, if I were about to act in any way not

* Ibid. s. 19, p. 123.

rightly. But now there has befallen me, as you yourselves see, that which men may think, and most men do account, to be the greatest of evils. And yet this morning, neither when I came from home did the sign from the God oppose itself, nor when I came up hither to the court of judgment, nor anywhere during the defence I was about to make; although in other speeches it has often restrained me in the very midst of speaking. But now in this affair it has not anywhere opposed me, either in any deed or word. What, then, do I suppose to be the cause? I will tell you. That which has happened to me seems to be a good thing; and if we think death to be an evil, we are in error. Of this I have a sure evidence; for it cannot be that the accustomed sign would not have opposed itself to me, if I were not about to do something which is good.'*

'Wherefore, O my judges, you ought to be of good hope about death; and to know this to be true, that no evil can happen to a good man, whether in life or in death; nor are his affairs neglected by the gods. Nor are my affairs at this time the result of chance. But this is clear to me, that it were better for me now to die, and to be set free from troubles. Wherefore the sign has in no-

* Ibid. s. 31, p. 164.

thing opposed me. I am, therefore, in no way angry
with those who have condemned me, nor with those
who have accused me; though they have condemned
and accused me with no good will, but rather with
the thought to hurt me. This, indeed, in them is
worthy of blame.'*

Such was his general defence against his accusers.
He stood up as a man conscious of something in him
higher than himself; of a calling and a mission to
his countrymen. He had laboured to recall them
from luxury, self-indulgence, ambition, civil strife,
political profligacy, and private corruption. He
told them roundly that no man could serve them
who mixed in their politics—that no man could
rebuke their corruptions and live.

Therefore it was that Meletus and Anytus accused him; and their accusation was the expression
of a wide-spread enmity in Athens.

The charges laid against Socrates were chiefly
two: the one, that of corrupting the youth of the
day by his philosophy; the other, that of impiety,
and of introducing new gods, ἕτερα καινὰ δαιμόνια,
or of denying the existence of gods. It is with the
latter we have chiefly to do, because it connects
itself with the belief of Socrates in respect to the

* Ibid. s. 33, p. 172.

Dæmonion, or voice, or sign, which from his childhood had been with him as a monitor and guide.

In answer to the charge of atheism, Socrates asked
his accuser: ' Is there any man who believes that
there are human affairs, but does not believe in the
existence of men ; or that there are certain rules for
managing horses, and yet believes that there is no
such thing as a horse ?   There is no such man.
But pray answer me this point: is there any man
who believes divine things and yet denies the being
of a God ?'   Meletus answered, 'No, certainly.'
Then Socrates replied : ' You acknowledge, then, that
I believe and teach the existence of Deities.   So
that, whether they be new or old, you still own that
I believe in divinities or divine agencies.   Now if I
believe that there are divinities or divine agencies,
I must necessarily suppose that there are Gods.' *

In these passages of Plato we have the fullest and
most explicit declaration of Socrates respecting the
Dæmon by which he was admonished.   He tells us
that it was ' a familiar sign: an oracle; a divine
voice :' that this sign had been with him from his
infancy: that its office was to take him off from
certain lines of action; that it did not impel him
to any.

* Ibid. s. 15, p. 105.

With such declarations before him, it is not
wonderful that Plutarch should have supposed this
Dæmon to be a personal being, and that he should
have written a book, ' De Genio Socratis,' on the
' Familiar Spirit of Socrates : ' and that Apuleius
should have written ' De Deo Socratis,' of ' The God
of Socrates : ' and that the Neoplatonists and certain
of the Christian Fathers should have understood this
Dæmonion to be a personal being or genius : whether
good or bad, they did not determine.

Plutarch has not promoted either the perspicuity
or the gravity of the subject by telling us that ' a
voice in the Cave of Trophonius expounded to
Timarchus the philosophy of dæmons in the following
words : " Every soul partakes of reason. It cannot
be without reason and intelligence. But so much
of each soul as is mixed with flesh and passions is
changed, and through pain or pleasure becomes
irrational. Every soul does not mix itself in the
same manner. For some plunge themselves altogether into the body, and so in this life their
whole frame is corrupted by appetite and passion ;
others are mixed only in part, but the purer part
still remains out of the body. It is not drawn down
into it ; but it floats above, and touches the upper
part of a man's head. It is like a cord to hold up

and direct the part of the soul which is sinking, as long as it proves obedient, and is not overcome by the passions of the flesh. The part that is plunged into the body is called the soul; but the uncorrupted part is called the mind, and people think that it is within them: as likewise they imagine the image reflected from a glass is in the glass. But the more intelligent, who know it to be external, call it a dæmon.' *

' Such was the soul of Hermodorus the Clazomenian, of which it is reported that for nights and days it would leave his body, travel over many countries, and return, after it had seen things and talked with persons at a great distance; till at last, by the treachery of his wife, his body was delivered to his enemies; and they burnt it in his own house while the soul was abroad.' Plutarch considerately adds : ' It is certain that this is not true;' but he goes on to say: ' The soul never went out of the body, but it loosened the tie that held the dæmon, and gave it range and freedom.' †

Plutarch then relates the following anecdote : ' More and greater things you may learn from Simias, and other companions of Socrates; but

* Plutarch, De Genio Socratis, sect. xxii. Moralia. Tom. i. 713. Ed. Dœhner, Paris, 1841.

† Ibid.

once, when I was present, as I went to Euthyphron
the soothsayer, it happened, Simias, as you remember, that Socrates was going up to Symbolum, and
the house of Andocides, all the way asking questions,
and playfully attacking Euthyphron. When, sud-
denly standing still, and making us to do the same,
he pondered with himself for some time. Then,
turning about, he walked through Trunkmakers'
Street, calling back his friends that walked before
him, affirming that it was because of his dæmon.
Many turned back, amongst whom I, holding Euthyphron, was one; but some of the youths, keeping
on the straight road, in order, as it were, to dis-
prove the dæmon of Socrates, took along with them
Charillus the piper, who came with me to Athens
to see Cebes. Now, as they were walking through
Sculptors' Street, near the court houses, a herd of
pigs, covered with mud, met them; and, being too
many for the street, and running against one another,
they upset some that could not get out of the way,
and dirtied others; and Charillus came home with
his legs and clothes very muddy; so that often, in
merriment, they would remember Socrates' dæmon,
wondering at its constant care of the man, and that
Heaven kept such a particular watch over him.'*

* Ibid. sect. x.

'I myself, Galaxidorus, have heard a Megarian, who had it from Terpsion, say that Socrates' dæmon was nothing else but the sneezing either of himself or of others; for if another sneezed, either before, behind him, or on his right hand, then he went on to do what he was about; but if on the left hand, he refrained from acting. One sort of his own sneezing confirmed him, whilst deliberating and not fully resolved; another stopped him when already about to act. But indeed it seems strange that if he used sneezing as his sign, he should not have told this to his friends, but should have said that it was a dæmon that hindered or enjoined him.'*

The following passage is more to our purpose. Plutarch says: 'The resolute impulses of Socrates seem to be both vigorous and firm, as springing from right principles and strong judgment. Therefore he, of his own will, lived in poverty all his life, though he had friends who would have been glad and willing to give to him; he would not give up philosophy, notwithstanding all the discouragements he met with; and at last, when his friends endeavoured and skilfully contrived his escape, he would not yield to their entreaties, nor withdraw from death, but maintained an inflexible mind in the

* Ibid. sect. xi.

last extremity. And surely these are not the actions
of a man whose designs, when once fixed, could be
altered by omens or sneezings; but of one who, by
some higher guidance and principle, is directed to
do right.'*

Plutarch then says that Socrates foretold the over-
throw of the Athenians in Sicily; and that in the
pursuit at Delium he, with Alcibiades and Laches,
escaped by Registe, while others who would not
follow him were overtaken and slain. This caused
the dæmon of Socrates to be much talked of in
Athens.

We may now dismiss these speculations, and come
back to Socrates, and learn from himself what he
understood and intended us to understand by his
Dæmon or Dæmonion.

But here again we are brought to a standstill.
We cannot interrogate Socrates himself. We can
only get to him by hearsay. Between him and us
stand Xenophon and Plato. It is, after all, Xenophon and Plato, not Socrates, who speak to us.
Worse than this, Xenophon and Plato do not agree
in what they tell us; and, worst of all, what they
tell us evidently takes form and colour from their
own minds. It may recall to us Sir Walter Scott's

---

* Ibid. sect. ix.

description in 'Kenilworth' of Blount and Raleigh sitting on the bench in the hall at Say's Court. They were both looking in silence at the wall. The bluff old soldier looked at the wall and saw the wall, and nothing but the wall; but between the wall and the eye of Sir Walter Wittypate there was a whole imaginary world, with an endless procession and maze of persons and things of his own creation.

The Socrates of Xenophon stands out clear, hard, definite; a matter of fact description, a photograph with few after-touches, with little sense that anything needs explanation, or could have any meaning but the letter of the text. The Socrates of Plato comes to us through the prisms of his marvellous imagination; so as to create a misgiving whether it be a conscientious likeness or a portrait by the hand of an artist and a friend, too creative and too fond to be faithful.

Nevertheless, we are reduced to those two biographers. They are the only full and trustworthy witnesses in close personal contact with the man whom they describe.

We will endeavour, then, to ascertain what they understood by the dæmon of Socrates. This will at least give the best approximation to what Socrates understood by it himself.

c

In order to do this, we will first take down their evidence as they give it, and next compare the two testimonies; and, lastly, make an estimate of their differences.

When this is done we may use our own criticism : for it is one thing to ascertain what Socrates may have understood, it is another to ascertain what we may understand by the psychological facts narrated by him or by them. It is not to be too hastily assumed that Socrates was an adequate interpreter of the internal facts even of his own mind. It is not unreasonable to believe that the philosophical and other profounder experience of two thousand years may have enabled us more truly than he could to analyse and to appreciate the facts and phenomena of moral and mental philosophy. The heart has beat, and the blood has circulated, from the beginning of time ; yet we take the physiology of Harvey as to the blood, rather than that of Hippocrates. The Ethics even of Aristotle are, in analytical depth and precise delineation, conspicuously in advance of the method and teaching of Socrates. In this the disciple is above his master, and we may be above both.

Let us begin then with Xenophon. The chief passages in which he describes the Dæmonion are as follows.

'It was in the mouths of men that Socrates declared that the Deity, or Dæmonion (τὸ δαιμόνιον) made things known to him, or gave him signs by which to know them.'

'He used to say that the Dæmonion signified (things) to him: and that he often advised those who were with him to do some things, and not to do others, as the Dæmonion forewarned him.' *

'For he thought that the Gods (τοὺς Θεοὺς) had care of men in a way unlike that which most men imagine: for they suppose that the Gods know indeed some things, and do not know others. But Socrates believed the Gods to know all things: whatsoever things are said, or done, or purposed in secret: and that they are everywhere present: and that they make known human things to men.' †

When Hermogenes sorrowfully upbraided him for not defending himself more elaborately, and for even provoking his judges against him, Socrates answered: 'Of a truth, Hermogenes, when I set to work to think out my defence before the judges the Dæmonion hindered me.' ‡

Finally, Xenophon says of him that he was 'so

---

* Xenoph. Mem. lib. i. c. 1, s. 1. Oxon. 1785.   † Ibid. s. 4.
‡ Ibid. lib. iv. c. 8, s. 3.

pious that he would do nothing without the counsel of the Gods.' *

Such then is the evidence of Xenophon : upon which these remarks may be made.

1. That Xenophon carefully distinguishes between the Dæmon of Socrates, which he calls τὸ δαιμόνιον, and the Gods, whom he calls τοὺς Θεούς.

2. That he describes the Dæmonion as showing beforehand what things are to be done, and what not to be done : that is to say, that the action of this monitor was both to enjoin and to forbid.

3. That he refers this admonition and direction to the Gods, without whose counsel (γνώμη) Socrates would never act.

4. That nothing in Xenophon is to be found which invests the Dæmonion with personality, or with any other character than that of a divine influence or agency, or a counsel or direction of the Gods acting upon the reason of man.

We will now proceed to our other witness.

The chief passages of Plato bearing on the Dæmonion are those which we have already quoted from the Apology. They need not be repeated.

To these may be added what follows.

In the Euthydemus, Socrates says : ' I happened to be providentially sitting alone in the place where

* Xenoph. Mem. lib. iv. c. 8, s. 4.

you saw me, in the dressing room (of the Lycæum), and I had in my mind to be gone. When I got up, the accustomed sign, the Dæmonion, came; I therefore again sat down.'* Soon after came Euthydemus and his companions.

Again, in the Phædrus: 'When I was about to cross the river, the Dæmonion, the accustomed sign, came, which restrains me when I am about to do anything; and I seemed to hear a certain voice, which did not suffer me to proceed until I should have expiated myself, as having in some way offended against God.'†

And in the Alcibiades, he says: 'The cause of this was nothing human, but a certain divine hindrance, the power of which you shall hereafter hear; but now, as it no longer hinders me, I am therefore come, and I am in good hope that for the future it will not hinder me.' ‡

In the Theætetus, he says: 'The Dæmonion which comes to me hinders my intercourse with some, and not with others.' §

And in the Republic: 'It is not worth while to speak of the divine sign which comes to me: whether it have occurred to any other or not.'||

I do not quote from the Theages, in which there

---

* Euthydemus, 273, vol. vi. p. 80. Ed. Stallbaum, Gothæ, 1836.
† Phædrus, 242, vol. iv. 72.   ‡ Alcibiades, 103, vol. v. 221.
§ Theætetus, 151, vol. viii. 71. || De Republica, lib. vi. s. 496.

is much on the point, for two reasons. First, doubts have been raised as to its authenticity : and secondly, the statements contained in it may be found also in other dialogues of which there is no doubt.

Now in these passages we have the following points :

1. That the Dæmonion is spoken of as θεῖον τί, δαιμόνιον, σημεῖον, φωνή, and εἰωθυῖα τοῦ δαιμονίου μαντική : something divine, something of the Deity, a sign, a voice, the accustomed divination or oracle of the Deity. It is evident, therefore, that Plato represents it as an agency, or a voice, not as an agent or a person ; and if the agent or person from whom this agency or voice proceed be sought for, it is to be found in God or in the Gods.

2. That the function of this agency or voice was to check, to hinder, and to restrain, not to suggest or to prompt to any line of action.

3. That it manifested itself in such apparently fortuitous events as the hindering the departure of Socrates from the Lycæum till Euthydemus came ; and πάνυ ἐπὶ σμικροῖς, even in the least things : that is to say, its function was to forewarn or to check in matters not so much of right and wrong as of safety, or of expediency, or of good fortune.

Comparing these two testimonies of Xenophon and Plato we find—

1. That they agree as to the impersonal nature of the Dæmonion. The terms used by them signify at the utmost a divine agency or a divine voice; they do not signify the presence or attendance of a divine person, or of a familiar spirit.

It is, perhaps, not wonderful that some of the ancients should have so misunderstood their language, and that Socrates should have been accused of introducing new deities. The same charge was in like manner made against the Apostle at Athens, because he preached the Resurrection, τὴν ἀνάστασιν. Nevertheless Cicero understood Plato's language, and translated the Dæmonion by ' divinum aliquid.'

It is to be borne in mind that both Xenophon and Plato speak, not as we do, of the Δαίμων of Socrates, but of the δαιμόνιον. They never speak of the δαιμόνιον as Θεός; but observe strictly the known distinction between these terms. Δαιμόνιον signifies the abstract or neuter idea of Divine power, the Deity, or the Divinity. As Aristotle says, it implies ἢ Θεὸς ἢ Θεοῦ ἔργον,* either the presence or the power, not of a δαίμων or inferior divinity, but of God. Δαίμων is so far used convertibly with Θεός, that it is sometimes used for Θεός, but Θεὸς is never used for Δαίμων. Θεὸς and Δαίμων are

* Arist. Rhet. ii. xxiii. 8.

sometimes used together; but Δαίμων signifies a divinity of lower rank.

In the Apology, Socrates tells his judges that when he was coming out of his house, τὸ τοῦ θεοῦ σημεῖον, the sign of the God, distinguishing the agency from the person, hindered him. Xenophon also makes Euthydemus say that the Gods showed a special friendship to Socrates. And again he says, speaking of voices, signs, and divinations, that by these things, τοὺς θεοὺς σημαίνειν, the Gods signified things to man. The δαιμόνιον was one of those signs: impersonal, derived from a divine agent.

2. That they disagree as to the function or office of the Dæmonion. Xenophon ascribes to it the twofold office of suggestion and restraint. Plato ascribes to it expressly that of restraint only.

Plutarch agrees with Xenophon, and describes its office as either restraining or enjoining; κωλύων ἤ κελεύων.*

3. That they further disagree, inasmuch as Xenophon recognises the action of the Dæmonion in matters of right or wrong, as well as in matters of expediency; whereas Plato seems to restrict it to the latter.

The sum of the evidence, therefore, may be thus

* De Genio Socratis, sect. xi.

stated. Socrates believed himself 'to be assisted from his childhood by a divine agency, whereby he was forewarned and guided in matters of his own personal conduct, both towards himself, as in his escape after the defeat at Delium, and his waiting in the Lycæum; and towards others, as in judging what disciples to receive or to reject, and in his whole mission as cross-examiner of his fellow-countrymen.

Such is the judgment of ancient writers. I will quote only a few of the many modern critics on this subject. Bishop Thirlwall says: 'Socrates, who was used to reflect profoundly on the state of his own mind, had, it seems, gradually become convinced that he was favoured by the Gods with an inward sign, which he described as a voice.' *

In like manner, Mr. Grote says: 'We have also to note that marked feature in the character of Socrates, the standing upon his own individual reason, and measure of good and evil; nay, even perhaps his confidence in it so far as to believe in a divine voice informing and moving him.' † Mr. Grote further refers in a note to a curious passage from the Life of Coriolanus by Plutarch, where he says that the Gods do not infuse into men new

* Hist. of Greece, vol. iv. p. 290. † Grote's Plato, vol. i. p. 295.

volitions; but they work upon the principle of
association in the mind, suggesting ideas which
conduct to the appropriate volitions. Plutarch's
words are—'Not infusing the motive powers, but
the ideas which call those motive powers into
activity; not making the act involuntary by con-
straint, but giving an outset to the will, and in-
spiring it with courage and hope.'*

According to both these estimates it would appear
that the groundwork of this divine action, as Socrates believed it to be, was the intellectual and moral
activity of his own mind.

Zeller, in his work on Socrates and the Socratic
Schools, gives his estimate of the Dæmonion in the
following words:—

'The δαιμόνιον is therefore an internal oracle, and
as such it is by Xenophon and Plato included under·
the more general notion of divination, and placed
on a par with divination by sacrifice and the flight
of birds. In attempting to bring this inward
revelation of Socrates into harmony with the facts
of psychology, it may be laid down in the first place
that the *dæmonium* must not be confounded with

---

* Κινοῦντα τὴν προαίρεσιν,'οὐδ' ὁρμὰς ἐνεργαζόμενον, ἀλλὰ φαντασίας
ὁρμῶν ἀγωγούς, αἷς οὐδὲ ποιεῖ τὴν πρᾶξιν ἀκούσιον, ἀλλὰ τῷ ἑκουσίῳ
δίδωσιν ἀρχὴν καὶ τὸ θαρρεῖν καὶ τὸ ἐλπίζειν προστίθησιν.   In Vita
M. Coriolani, vol. i. sect. xxxiii. Ed. Dœhner.   Paris, 1857.

the voice of conscience, as many ancient and modern critics have done.' . . . 'The δαιμόνιον has nothing to do with the universal moral standard, which, according to Socrates, is a matter for pure intelligence to determine.' . . . 'For these [that is, actions in prospect] Socrates either has recourse to μαντική in general, or to his δαιμόνιον, leaving moral conduct to be determined by clear knowledge.' *

We are here approaching to the estimate which appears to me to be both adequate and true.

Mr. Riddell of Balliol, after carefully analysing the evidence we have hitherto examined, says :—

'If, then, declining Socrates' account, we are disposed to refer the phenomenon to ordinary psychological causes, we can do so satisfactorily, provided we confine our attention to Xenophon's account alone. All Xenophon's notices of it encourage the view that it was a quick exercise of a judgment, informed by knowledge of the subject, trained by experience, and inferring from cause to effect, without consciousness of the process. In a mind so purified by temperance and self-knowledge, so single of purpose, and unperturbed by lower aims, endowed with such powerful natural faculties, especially those

* Zeller's Socrates and the Socratic Schools, pp. 76-78. Longman, 1868.

of observation and of causality, the ability to forecast and forejudge might become almost an immediate sense.'

'As to the reconcilement of authorities, when Plato makes Socrates say, ἀεὶ ἀποτρέπει με, he describes it by its most perceptible act. For its coincidence with an existing purpose would be superfluous and little noticeable.' . . . 'The voice was no impulse: it did not speak to the will, but had a critical or reflexive function.'

Mr. Riddell goes on to say, that the δαιμόνιον was 'an unanalysed act of judgment;' that it was κριτική, not ἐπιτακτική, that it was Socrates' substitute for μαντική, and that, where men are wont to have recourse to external preternatural aids, Socrates went by a guide within himself: that to this guide he, in all good faith, gave a religious name. 'His mental acts, so far as he could unravel them, were his own, were human : beyond his ken, they were divine; and what really was of the nature of an immediate critical sense, seemed to him an immediate inspiration.' *

This appears to me to be in outline an explanation both true and adequate.

If I were asked to add my own judgment as to

* Riddell's Apology of Plato, pp. 105-8. Oxford, 1867.

what the Dæmon of Socrates was, in the estimate of Socrates himself, I should answer as follows :—

It was a belief of a divine assistance, granted, as he says, to all men in some things, and in some special circumstances; of which most men are hardly, if at all, conscious : but in his case it was consciously recognised from his childhood, and it acted upon him in and through the intellectual and moral operations of his own mind : so that he ascribed to the action of the Dæmonion much that was undoubtedly the normal activity of his own intellectual and moral state.

Such, I think, Socrates believed it to be.

If, however, I were asked what we may believe it to have been, I would answer :—

1. That, holding altogether with Lord Bacon, when he says in his 'Essay on Atheism,' 'I had rather believe all the fables of the Legend, and the Talmud, and the Alcoran, than that this universal frame is without a mind '—we may well believe in a divine providence surrounding the life, and a divine action present to the mind, of any man who, according to the testimony of one that knew him by closest intimacy, was 'so pious as never to do anything without the counsel of the Gods; so just as never to hurt anyone even in the lightest thing:

but full of the greatest benefit to all who conversed
with him : so temperate as never to prefer what was
pleasant to what was best : so prudent as never to
err in discerning the better from the worse ; and
never to need the judgment of any other in this
discernment, being sufficient in himself.' *   That a
divine providence and a divine help are over the
whole intellectual and moral world, is an axiomatic
truth in the relation of God to man : that they
may be looked for in a special degree in just and
prudent men, follows as a corollary from that axiom.
But as this lies beyond our analysis, we will confine ourselves to the subject as a matter of
psychology.

I will therefore add a further proposition, namely:

2. That the statements of Xenophon and Plato
may be, not only harmonised, but brought under the
same psychological explanation, resting on the laws
of the speculative and the practical reason.   It
would indeed be too narrow an explanation, as
Zeller objects, to refer the signs of this monitor to
the action of conscience alone; for conscience is
only one office, or one function, of the reason of
man.   Nevertheless it is certain, that in a large part
of that which Socrates referred to the Dæmonion,

* Xenoph. Memorabilia, lib. iv. c. 8, s. 5.

conscience was directly present and perceptibly in action. It is no objection to this to quote, as Zeller does, the declaration of Socrates that, ' It is idle to consult the Gods about things which may be known by deliberation,'* or to say that Socrates ' referred morals to the judgment of reason.'† This is precisely the philosophical definition of conscience. Conscience is *dictamen rationis*. It is reason acting upon right and wrong with a view to practice : just as apprehension is the reason acting upon truth and falsehood with a view to science. In matter of speculative truth, as in physical science, geometry, and the like, the intellect acts without any response from the passions or affections of the moral nature. Aristotle in the ' Rhetoric' says that mathematics have no ethical character, but that the teaching of Socrates has.‡ In matter of practical truth, the discernments of the intellect are followed by a response of the moral nature by way of approval or disapproval. But the *primary* judge is the reason, the response of the moral nature is *secondary*. It is, therefore, most true that morals are subject to the jurisdiction of reason ; but that does not prove that this monitor of Socrates was not in great part the action of conscience.

* Ibid. p. 78.   † Ibid.   ‡ Rhet. iii. 16, 8.

And here it may be well to make more clear and precise the philosophical definition of conscience.

Scientia is the simple knowledge of things by the reason. *Conscientia* is the self-knowledge of the reason or mind. 'Nil conscire sibi, nulla pallescere culpa.' Now this conscience in its *first* intention is consciousness, as we commonly call it. It extends over all the internal acts of the reason or mind, over the whole inner world of our personal identity. Conscience, in the *second* intention of common parlance, signifies the reason judging of moral action, and discerning of right from wrong, with an approval or disapproval of the moral sense following upon its decisions. Metaphysicians, therefore, distinguish the operations of conscience into two kinds, and speak of a *psychological* conscience, by which we reflect upon internal acts of the mind in general, and a *moral* conscience, by which we reflect upon and judge of the *ethical* character of actions, whether internal or external. And this conscience they again distinguish into *habitual* and *actual.* The *habitual* conscience is the permanent disposition of the mind in relation to its own moral *state*; the *actual* conscience is the exertion of its attention and judicial discernment on its own moral *acts.* The *habitual* conscience is *spontaneous*, and therefore unconscious; the *actual* conscience is reflex, *deliberate*, and therefore conscious.

Such is the language of scholastic philosophy; and this seems with great precision to account for the fact which Socrates appears to have observed in himself, and Plato has recorded; namely, that the Dæmonion seemed to act only by way of check and restraint. The spontaneous action of conscience was habitual and unperceived; the actual aroused attention and conscious effort.*

In saying, then, that this internal monitor of Socrates is the reason, including the conscience, I intend expressly to include what is here described as the psychological as well as the moral conscience, and also the distinction between the habitual or spontaneous, and the actual or deliberate conscience. The application of this will be further seen when we answer an objection which may be anticipated. This comprehensive view includes all the mental judgments, whether of expediency or of morality, that is, both of prudence and of rectitude.

As to the examples given by Xenophon and Plato, in almost every one of them may be traced a moral element and a moral discernment.

---

* Prisco. Filosofia Speculativa, tom. i. pp. 208–10. Napolis, 1864.

For instance: The decision of Socrates to keep out of politics, that he might better serve the public good. This is surely a high moral judgment, involving the noblest motives of relative duty. The discernment as to what disciples to retain, or what persons to receive back again among them after they had once left him, unless it were a blind and capricious act, which in Socrates is incredible, must have been founded upon such a discernment of moral qualities and distinctions, both in his own character and in that of others, as to demand the exercise of the moral reason. When we say that one man is *simpatico* and another *antipatico*, we are exercising a moral sense and discrimination of an intimate and explicit sort; and this determines us in receiving or refusing to receive men to our confidence.

In deciding that he would not defend himself so as to escape death, the action of conscience, sustaining the highest aspirations and the noblest intrepidity, is clearly revealed.

I admit that in the escape after the flight and pursuit at Delium, and in the waiting in the Lycæum, and in the matter of Plutarch's pigs, there is to be discerned rather the activity of prudence than of conscience. But on the supposition

THE DÆMON OF SOCRATES.

that the monitor of Socrates was a mature and experienced reason, the action of both prudence and conscience would be alike included.

To this it may be objected, that Plato distinctly declares that the monitor of Socrates told him, not what things to do, but what things not to do; that inasmuch as conscience has a two-fold office towards both good and evil, the Dæmonion could not be conscience.

But to this objection two answers may be made.

The first, that Xenophon and Plutarch directly say that the Dæmonion both enjoined and forbade, that is, pronounced for or against certain lines of action.

The other answer has been anticipated by the statements of our Scholastic Philosophy. It has been shown that the action of conscience, when it suggests or approves anything, is less perceptible than when it disapproves or forbids. This may be seen by analogies. We are insensible of our continuous respiration, but distinctly sensible of the act of holding the breath; it is an *actus imperatus* requiring a conscious exertion of the will. Again, in walking, we are unconscious of the momentum of our pace, but conscious of any hindrance, and even of the act of stopping. The moral reason or conscience is always in activity, but with little or no reflex action upon itself, until something offends it. We are then conscious of a change of attitude, and of a recoil. For instance, the reason and conscience of Socrates permitted him freely to mix among men to cross-examine them, but not to enter into politics. In the former, he followed his own spontaneous inclination; in the latter, he imposed a conscious restraint upon himself. This is what Aristotle describes as prudence, or Φρόνησις. He distinguishes it from science, as being an intellectual habit conversant with practical and contingent matter; and from intuition, as being of details rather than of principles. He says that Φρόνησις, or prudence, is an intellectual virtue conversant about moral action. And he ascribes to it a power of sight, which is so trained and perfected by experience as to discern with an intuitive rapidity what is right or expedient in practice. He says that prudent men have a faculty which men call (δεινότης) skill, or ability, or resource, 'the nature of which is to do—and to do correctly—the things which conduce to the end proposed. If this aim be good, the skill is praiseworthy; but if it be bad, it becomes craft.' Wherefore Aristotle says, 'we call prudent men skilful, and not crafty. But prudence

is not the same as this faculty (i.e., δεινότης, or skill).
But the habit of prudence grows upon this *eye*, as
it were, of the soul.'* This is a precise description
of the prompt and provident intuition, a sort of
ἀγχίνοια, and εὐβουλία, presence of mind, rapidity of
counsel, with which Socrates discovered the useful,
or the expedient in matters of practice. But the
nature of this intellectual faculty is, in the main,
distinctly moral ; and belongs to the region of
conscience, or the discernment of right and wrong.

This instinct or faculty of moral discernment is
traceable throughout the whole history of the ancient
world. St. Paul only affirms what all records of
antiquity demonstrate in saying, ' When the Gentiles
which have not the law do by nature the things
contained in the law, these, having not the law, are a
law unto themselves, which show the works of the
law written in their hearts, their conscience also
bearing witness (συμμαρτυρούσης αὐτῶν τῆς συνειδη-
σέως), and their thoughts the meanwhile accusing or
else excusing one another.' †

Once more: it may be objected that it is not for
us to theorise as to what Socrates ought to have
understood of his own inward life, but to take
things as he expressed them.

* Arist. Eth. N. L. vi. xii. τῷ ὄμματι τούτῳ · γίνεται τῆς ψυχῆς.
† Rom. ii. 14, 15.

To this I have already by anticipation made one sufficient answer. But I will add another. Socrates refused to be classed with the philosophers or teachers of Athens. He delivered no system of philosophy. He framed to himself no moral or mental science. He found philosophy in the hands of physicists, or physical theorists, and of Sophists. He thought the Physicists to be vainly curious, if not impious, in trying to discover what the Gods kept secret: he thought the Sophists to be venal, superficial, and immoral. He was the founder, not of a new philosophy, but of a new era in philosophy. He extricated the conceptions of God and of morality from the region and philosophy of matter, and set them in the sphere of mind. He brought down philosophy, as Cicero says, from heaven to earth, to the market-place, and the streets, and the homes and the hearts of men. He cross-examined every man he met with, politicians, philosophers, rhetoricians, painters, private citizens, artizans: but he framed no system, and laid down no theories; he made no analysis of the human mind. Lord Bacon is said to have created a Novum Organum in philosophy by questioning Nature. This Socrates certainly did by questioning man. His method was one of universal questioning, whereby he heaped up materials for his disciples, one of whom afterwards gave to them a scientific order and precision of expression which has formed the imperishable basis of mental and moral philosophy to this day. The Ethics of Aristotle analyse, lay out, distinguish, and define the intellectual and moral processes of the human mind—modern metaphysicians must bear with me—with a truth which has never been surpassed. What Socrates felt, Aristotle has fixed by exact analysis. The character of Socrates is the φρόνιμος of Aristotle, the prudent man; but prudence is etymologically and essentially far-seeing,* the perfection of the moral reason. 'All men,' he says, 'seem to testify that such a habit which is according to prudence is virtue. But it is necessary to make a slight difference, for virtue is not only a habit according to right reason, but inseparably joined with right reason; and prudence is the same as right reason on these subjects. Socrates therefore,' Aristotle says, 'thought the virtues to be reasons or rational habits, for he thought them all to be sciences, but we think them to be intellectual habits joined with reason. It is clear, however, from what has been said, that it is impossible for a man to be properly virtuous without

* Prudens futuri temporis exitum
Caliginosa nocte premit Deus.—Hor. Od. iii. 29.

prudence, or to be prudent without moral virtue.' *
Aristotle seems to me to give in this passage the
psychological analysis of the intuition and providence with which Socrates was eminently endowed.
His prudence or φρόνησις constituted the αὐτάρκεια,
or self-dependence of reason in all questions of morality, of which Xenophon speaks.

> Nullum numen abest si sit Prudentia, nos te ,
> Nos facimus, Fortuna, deam cœloque locamus. †

The prudence of Socrates was his own moral state,
and yet *non sine Numine*, for we may well believe
that to him was granted no common share in the
'Light that lighteth every man that cometh into
this world.'

In saying this, I am not rejecting the supposition
that the particular providence which never suffers
even a sparrow to fall to the ground without its
Creator's will, may have in a special way encompassed
the life of a man who witnessed in a corrupt world to
the lights of nature and to the laws of right.   In the
midst of an intellectual frivolity and a moral degra-
dation never surpassed in the history of mankind,
made all the guiltier by reason of the refined culture

* Eth. N. L. vi. xiii.
† Juvenal, lib. iv. sat. x. 365-6.

and luxurious civilization of Athens, Socrates bore witness, until seventy years of age, to the supremacy of prudence, justice, fortitude, and temperance, the four perfections of man in the order of nature.

Whether the estimate I have given of the Dæmonion of Socrates be true or not, the inquiry in which we have been engaged is manifestly not a barren speculation. It sets before us a great moral example, it teaches us a great moral law, necessary to men at all times, vital to us in these declining days. I mean, that there is no way for men to attain their true dignity, nor to serve their age and country, but to be upright in conscience, and even at the cost of life to be both in public and private duty prudent and temperate, just and brave. It tells us with a thrilling human voice, and in the accents of our common humanity, that man's supreme rule of right is the moral reason or conscience; that the cultivation of the mere intellect, while the moral life and powers lie fallow, is the work of sophists, deceivers, or deceived, or both ; that the education of man is his moral formation; that intellectual culture without moral goodness is a wildfire and a pestilence which makes havoc of men and states ; that knowledge is virtue, and virtue knowledge ; for that, unless we would maim and mutilate our being, the intellectual and moral powers of man must be simultaneously and equably unfolded and matured. These are axioms of the moral life; vital, I say, at all times and in all lands, but nowhere more in season and more wholesome than to us who, in the sudden growth of a vast maritime empire, splendid and unstable for its very greatness, in the refinements of luxury, and the inundation of a stupendous prosperity, seem to be developing some of the moral and intellectual evils which went before the fall of imperial Athens;— political factions, licentious freedom, sophistical education, a relaxation of moral and religious traditions, a growing scepticism, an unstable public opinion swayed to and fro by nameless hands, and by irresponsible voices. In such a public state Socrates lived and died, bequeathing to us this lesson—that Conscience is the Voice of God.

LONDON: PRINTED BY
SPOTTISWOODE AND CO., NEW-STREET SQUARE
AND PARLIAMENT STREET

www.ingramcontent.com/pod-product-compliance
Lightning Source LLC
Chambersburg PA
CBHW021246260626
47172CB00002B/851